Foundation

www.theabilitiesinme.com
Registered Charity No: 1197965

This book is inspired by Louie George Wood, age 6 with Cerebral Palsy.

This book also features Louie Oscar Black, age 3, Cayden Kidou Hyun-Myung Lee, age 7 and Chanel Murrish, age 8.

Published in association with Bear With Us Productions

© 2021 Gemma Keir
The Abilities In Me - Cerebral Palsy

www.theabilitiesinme.com

ISBN: 9798421733850

Edited by Emma Lusty and Claire Bunyan
Illustrated by Yevheniia Lisovaya

www.justbearwithus.com

The abilities in me

Cerebral Palsy

Written by Gemma Keir

Illustrated by Yevheniia Lisovaya

I would like to tell you a story
about my condition, which you may see.

It is something I was diagnosed with and it's called cerebral palsy.

Cerebral palsy is a group of disorders.
Cerebral relates to our brain.
Palsy is what makes our muscles weak,
which can sometimes cause us pain.

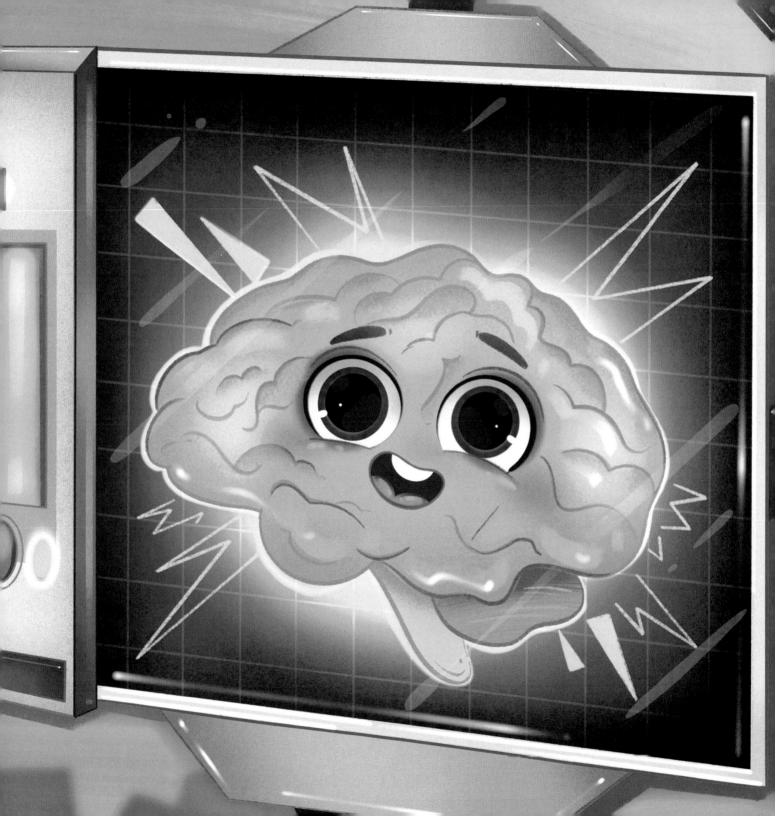

It can be due to being born early,
lack of oxygen or an infection.
It could be caused by a stroke or low blood sugar,
cerebral palsy is a broad spectrum.

It can be diagnosed from an early age,
when symptoms start to appear.
You may find it hard to walk, eat or talk,
feel wobbly, stiff or not see as clear.

There are so many children with cerebral palsy;
it affects everyone in a different way.
Here is a list of the different types, please take a

LOOK AT THE NEXT PAGE

Quadriplegia
All four limbs (whole body) are affected

Dyskinetic
Muscles are stiff and floppy

Hemiplegia
One side of the body is affected

Diplegia
Two limbs are affected

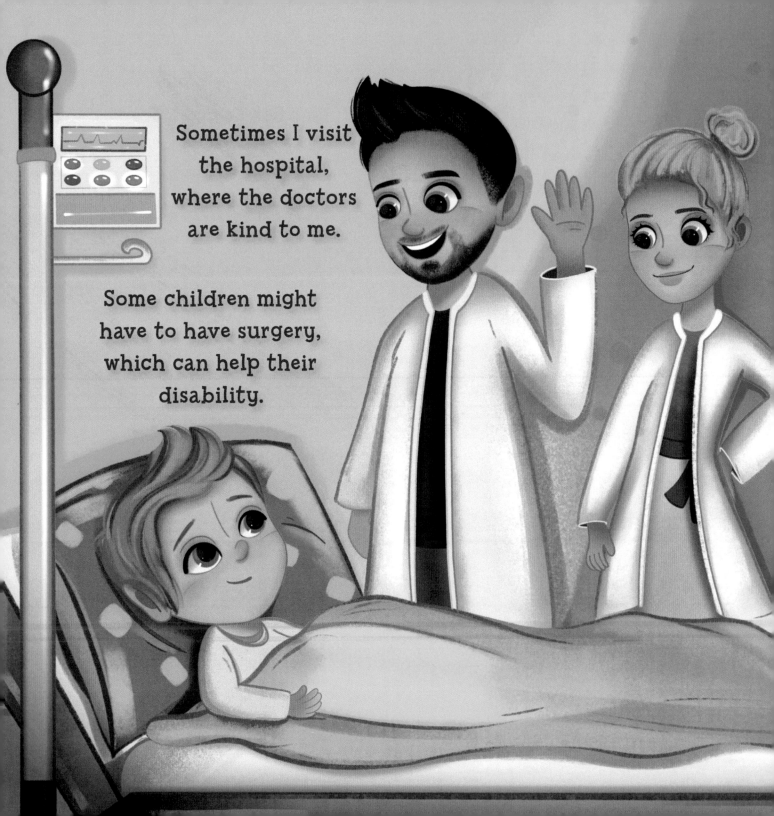

Sometimes I visit the hospital, where the doctors are kind to me.

Some children might have to have surgery, which can help their disability.

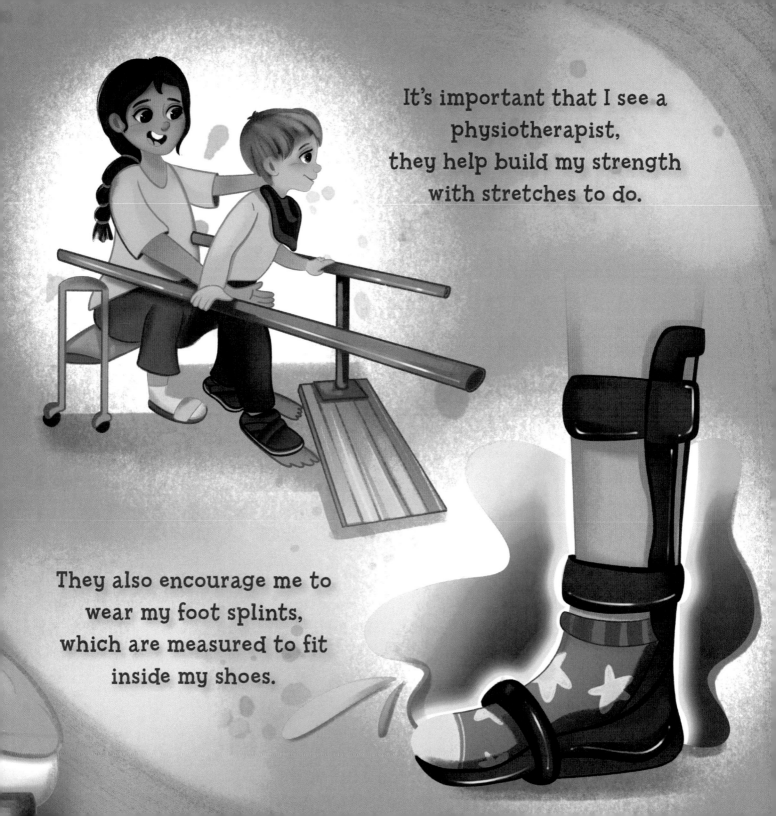

It's important that I see a
physiotherapist,
they help build my strength
with stretches to do.

They also encourage me to
wear my foot splints,
which are measured to fit
inside my shoes.

Some children with cerebral palsy,
need special equipment to help them move.
Crutches, a walker, a stick or a wheelchair
are a few of the things we might use.

I like to use my adaptive bicycle,
when I go outside on a sunny day.
I have to make sure I wear my helmet,
to keep me safe whilst I play.

When I see my
speech therapist,
they always bring
fun things to do.

We look through pictures
and they help me to sign,
I can use a device to
communicate too!

Some children might drool or
have trouble eating
and need softer food instead.

Doctors and therapists can really help,
you may see some children tube fed.

There are so many things
I love about school,
like the sensory room
where I can play.

Reading stories and
listening to music,
are always a fun
part of my day.

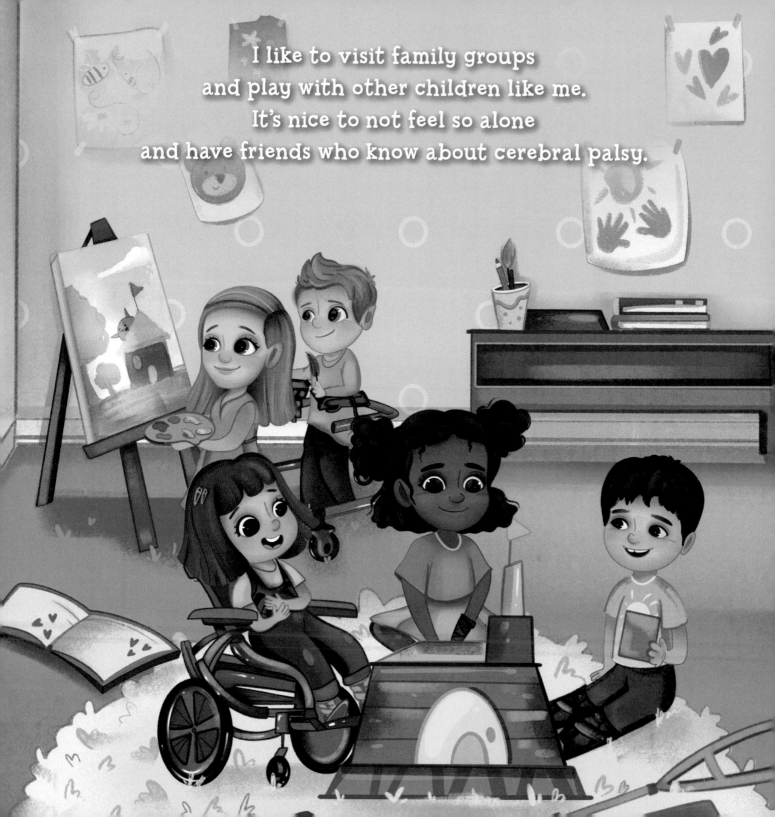

I like to visit family groups
and play with other children like me.
It's nice to not feel so alone
and have friends who know about cerebral palsy.

I love to be with my family,
they make me feel super cool!
Hydrotherapy helps my muscles relax,
I have so much fun when we visit the pool.

When we are together at home,
I like to watch football and roar!

And when I stand up with my walker,
I can kick a ball across the floor.

When the day is finally over,
I get supported into bed.
My family come over to say goodnight
and they kiss me on the head.

So now you know I have cerebral palsy
and the things I love to do.
Let's be friends and you can tell me,
what abilities are in you?

Write down your Super Abilities!

What makes you Happy?
Please draw below!

Support Information

Originally established in 1954, BDCPS is a small charity based in Bedfordshire, which provides playschemes and youth clubs for children and young people with complex disabilities (aged 0 to 25). In addition BDCPS also provide critical support and wellbeing activities to families, which includes parent carers and siblings. Our parent carer wellbeing provision continues to grow and develop and we offer a variety of sessions to support parents and carers with their own wellbeing. At BDCPS we focus on ABILITY rather than disability. We go to great lengths to ensure all clubs are inclusive, creative, inspiring and empowering! BDCPS provide specialist support for those living with Cerebral Palsy in Bedford Borough and Central Bedfordshire. As well as Cerebral Palsy, we are there to support and help provide services, support and activities for a huge range of disabilities, many of which are life limiting. All our youth clubs and playschemes provide young people with 1:1 support and our professional team of staff who are trained to meet all care needs.

www.bdcps.charity
Contact: 01234 351759

✉ cp.enquiries@bdcps.org.uk
🅕 🅞 🐦 @bdcps

Support Information

A registered nonprofit charity focused on helping individuals with cerebral palsy and other disabilities in the province of Saskatchewan, Canada. Our mission is to ensure individuals with cerebral palsy have the right to opportunities to achieve their fullest potential, through education health care and access to all amenities of the community.

Reg Charity #1191139921RR0001

2310 Louise Avenue
Saskatoon, Saskatchewan S7J 2C7
Phone (306) 955 - 7272

www.cpsk.ca

✉ cerebralpalsysask@gmail.com
f www.facebook.com/Saskcp
🐦 www.twitter.com/SaskCp
📷 www.instagram.com/cpsaskatchewan
in www.linkedin.com/company/cerebral-palsy-saskatchewan

Support Information

Our mission statement – "To enable, inspire and support children with cerebral palsy and their families"

Contact Addresses:
3 Croxteth Avenue, Wallasey, Wirral, CH44 5UL
Tudor Hall, York Street, Runcorn, WA7 5BB

www.sticknstep.org

⬤ www.facebook.com/sticknstep.charity
⬤ www.twitter.com/SticknStep1

The only UK charity dedicated to supporting those touched by HIE (Hypoxic-Ischaemic Encephalopathy), a lack of oxygen/blood flow to the brain.

Contact: 0800 987 5422
Text/Call: 07838 197 945

www.peeps-hie.org

✉ info@peeps-hie.org

⬤⬤⬤ @PeepsHIE
Download our free app, Peeps HIE

Support Information

Cerebral Palsy
ALLIANCE
RESEARCH FOUNDATION

We are the foremost organization in the world that solely focuses on cerebral palsy (CP) research. CP is the most common lifelong physical disability in the world and it is one of the most underfunded. We will be the ones to change that. We find, fund, and support the researchers who positively reshape what it's like to live with CP. CPARF will change that through strategic funding directed to five research priorities:

- **Early detection and early intervention**
- **Chronic pain**
- **Technology**
- **Regenerative medicine**
- **Genomics**

CP was once thought of as unchangeable and we're changing the way people think.

www.cparf.org

www.facebook.com/ResearchForCP
www.instagram.com/researchforcp

The Abilities in Me Foundation aims to raise awareness of special educational needs and conditions that children may encounter. We have an ever-growing book series written for young people that celebrates what these children can do, rather than what they cannot do. The Foundation also provides community support through forums and special events and works with schools to deliver educational workshops.

At the Abilities in Me, we want all children, regardless of their barriers to feel accepted and understood. The books are inspired by real children and experiences and they enable parents and teachers to talk about different needs and conditions with their children in a fun, safe and engaging way.

Our book series has had such a positive impact on children around the world and we will continue to widen our range and encourage further research and funding into different conditions. The Abilities in Me Foundation aims to raise funds to support worthy causes and by bringing awareness into schools, we hope that this will encourage kindness and reduce bullying.

Registered Charity No: 1197965

Find out more information via our website **www.theabilitiesinme.com**
 @theabilitiesinmebookseries

Check out our bookshelf!

    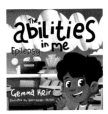

   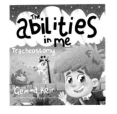 

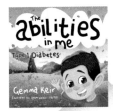 

available at

Made in the USA
Las Vegas, NV
22 October 2024

10322281R00026